Cotswold Pub Walks

by
Colin Handy

Twenty circular Pubwalks exploring the countryside between
Cotswold Pubs.

Walks taken from the Gloucestershire Citizen's popular
"Shanks's Pony" series of Pubwalks.

REARDON & SON
CHELTENHAM, ENGLAND

Published
by
REARDON PUBLISHING
56, Upper Norwood Street, Leckhampton,
Cheltenham, Glos, GL53 0DU, England
Website: www.reardon.co.uk

Copyright © 1995
REARDON & SON

2nd Edition 1999
Reardon Publishing

Written and researched by Colin Handy

Copyright © 1995
Colin Handy

ISBN 1 873877 15 3

Edited by Hilary Allison
Front Cover and Maps by Colin Handy

Photographs by Julia Craig

Illustrations by Peter Reardon
Layout and Design by Nicholas Reardon

Printed by
Stoate & Bishop (Printers) Ltd,
Cheltenham

INTRODUCTION

Cotswold Pubwalks

Someone once described the "Cotswolds" as the place that English exiles dream of when they dream of home.

For nowhere else in England offers its unique blend of chocolate box villages, built out of honey coloured stone, set in the greenest of backdrops.

"Wolds" is an old Saxon word meaning uplands, yet these are uplands with hardly a hill in sight; a place where the walking is easy and a friendly village pub is never far away. Most are traditional pubs with open fireplaces and blackened beams, places where "real ale" is always on tap to complement a "ploughman's platter".

This book is dedicated to those pubs and features twenty short and easy walks to help guide you there.

Whether you are young or old, walking alone or with your family, these walks will open your eyes to a Cotswold landscape that cries out to be walked, whatever the season.

COLIN HANDY

THE COUNTRY CODE

* Guard against all risk of fire
* Fasten all gates
* Keep dogs under proper control
* Avoid damaging fences, hedges and walls
* Keep to paths across farmland
* Leave no litter
* Safeguard water supplies
* Protect wildlife, wild plants and tree
* Go carefully on country roads
* Respect the life of the countryside

Waymarking colour code:
* Blue Arrows - bridleway
* Yellow Arrows - footpaths only

WHEREVER YOU ROAM IN THE COUNTRY, FOLLOW THE CODE!

WALK 1

Andoversford to Foxcote

Distance: 4 miles

Allow: 2 1/2 hour

"A most pleasant, easy circular walk along paths which are, in the main, simple to follow and a pleasure to be on. A walk that takes in two pretty villages, three pubs and two shops."

This walk starts in Station Road, Andoversford where it is a simple task to find on-road parking. Here too is a Post Office and a small general store where you can stock up on provisions for the walk.

Andoversford is typical of many Cotswold villages in as much as it is very difficult to find its original heart as it grows with new houses and small commercial enterprises.

Begin your walk by setting off back towards the village centre, past the cattle market on your right and turn right into Gloucester Road, which serves as a part of the A436.

At the junction you pass over a brook and need to cross the road at this point to the "Royal Oak" public house, which you might want to visit before starting your journey or at the end. It's a nice old pub with open fires and serves "real ales", morning coffee, meals and snacks.

Follow the slope out of the village until you have the primary school on your right and turn left on a well marked " bridle way" which passes through two imposing metal gates. The way is flat and easy walking through an avenue of trees and already a wonderful view begins to open up to your left.

You are now walking parallel with the busy A40 Cheltenham to Oxford road and despite the annoying drum coming from it, you could in fact be a million miles from it and in the heart of the country. Soon you pass a majestic farmhouse on your left and continue straight ahead on the "bridle way" to cross the main A436 road.

Your way lies slightly to your left and is again signed as a "bridle way". However the famous "Frogmill Hotel" is just two minutes walk away on your left and might well tempt you to divert for a short break!

The path now has become a wide dirt track; continue straight ahead passing a barn on your right. Here there is a new golf course - a sight which is becoming an all too familiar on the Cotswolds. Here too is a fine view to your right of the village of Foxcote which is your next destination.

There are sheep all around as you follow the path towards the farm buildings on the top of the hill. The way here can get a little wet so come well prepared for this walk with appropriate footwear. Eventually the track improves as you follow it straight ahead past some renovated farm cottages on your right and fields stocked with "Jacob" sheep.

When the path meets a narrow country road, cross it with great care, as it can get busy and continue straight ahead on a well marked track towards the farm buildings at the top of the hill. This is once again easy walking with panoramic views in all directions.

After about 250 yards turn right where the yellow arrows mark the path towards a copse. Follow this broad path, keeping the dry stone wall on your left, and pass the copse. This really is a pretty spot and very peaceful. Go through a gate and take your direction across the field from the yellow arrow mark as it points you towards Foxcote, which is slightly to your right. Use as a marker the "Kilkenny Inn" which is on the hilltop ahead.

4

Cross the field, go through a gate and continue to follow the arrows in exactly the same direction as you have been walking towards the nearest two houses. The footpath passes to the left of these buildings and brings you out on a road, where you turn left. Follow the road into the village, which is home to some very attractive cottages. Keep the brook on your left and stay on the road as it sweeps right and begins to climb up hill.

Again you are blessed with a wonderful view to your left as you climb the gentle slope and emerge once again onto the busy A436 which you need to cross with great care. You are directly opposite the "Kilkenny Inn" which is a most splendid pub offering just about everything for the tired walker.

To continue the walk, go down the narrow road marked Dowdeswell to the left of the pub. The views from here are very different as the back of Cleeve Common opens up and there is a lovely view of the grand house, "Sandywell Park".

Continue down the hill, past "Allington House" to a crossroads which you go straight over towards Whittington. Now immediately leave the road and enter the first field on your right, where there is a footpath sign, and walk down the gentle slope of the field.

This last part is difficult to follow but keep straight ahead, enter a second field and press on until you come to a large Cotswold stone wall where you turn right to keep the wall on your left. When the wall ends turn right and after 20 yards cross the stile on your left.

This little piece can be wet and difficult but cross it with care to the second stile which you cross and turn to your right. Now keep the brook on your right as you walk the final short section back to Station Road and your car.

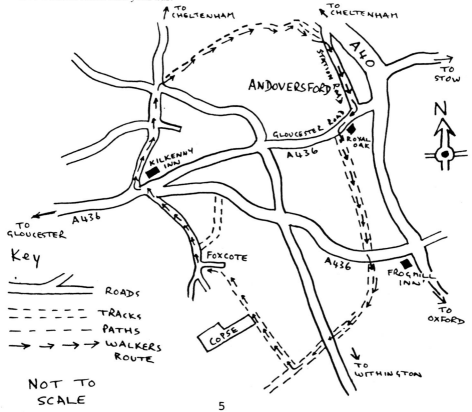

Key

ROADS
TRACKS
PATHS
WALKERS ROUTE

NOT TO SCALE

5

WALK 2

Ashleworth to Ashleworth Quay

Distance: 2 1/2 miles

Allow: 2 hours

"An easy, short walk, in and out of a real old village with its green, Preaching Cross and two old world pubs. A chance to combine meadows with river views and ancient buildings".

Remember, before you start this walk that Ashleworth lies on low land near river level and, depending upon the season, parts of this short walk can get wet and muddy - so wear appropriate footwear!

Your journey starts right in the centre of Ashleworth village somewhere near the pub, the "Queen's Arms". You already have a difficult decision to make, whether to visit the traditional old pub now or when you finish. It's a "free house", offering both a wide range of food and of course, "real ales".

Ashleworth is a mix of old and new houses with a village green and stone Preaching Cross.

Start the walk by heading back towards the green and pass the cross on your left. You are walking for a few minutes on the road to Hartpury and as it meanders, first right and then left, need to exercise care as it is narrow and quite well used.

After a quarter of a mile, turn left into Longridge Lane which is a "no through road" and you start to leave the village behind. It is a narrow, high hedged lane which, depending upon the time of year can be quite colourful and very rustic. Already you are deep into the countryside; it is very peaceful and the walking is easy.

After passing "Longridge Farm" the track can get very muddy as it peters out at a gate where you leave the track and follow the "bridle way" signs off to the left. If you are walking with children keep an eye on them at this point as you have a brook on your left covered in green slime which is most uninviting.

You are now walking towards the river in a flat, green valley. Behind you are grass banked hillocks, dotted with old farm buildings and scattered with orchards. Here is a scene untouched by time and for all the world you could be a million miles from Gloucester.

At the River Severn turn left through a gate and follow the line of the river bank, now on your right. The Severn at this point is wide, murky and in full flow as it forces its way against the incoming tide to the Bristol Channel and the awaiting sea.

Cross a series of stiles along this short section to Ashleworth Quay and your next port of call, the unforgettable hostelry, the "Boat Inn".

Here is an opportunity to stop for a pint and a snack in a pub that is truly "period". A flagstone passageway leads you through an old stable door into a bar straight out of a Laurie Lee novel." Real ales" are gently coaxed out of angled barrels and bottles of every kind fight for attention in an area where space is a premium.

When the weather is good, the walled pub garden comes alive with the excited chatter of walker, cyclist and trade, both from the road and the river.

Leave the pub and walk up the narrow road away from the river to pass an ancient "Tithe" barn, the property of "The National Trust" and still in daily use. The barn was built at the end of the 15th Century and is a ten bay barn with a stone tiled roof. Behind it lay two equally old buildings, "Ashleworth Court" and the Parish Church.

The court, built in 1460 of blue lias stone, was originally thatched and is an exceptionally complete medieval house which still boasts a "Great Hall" and although privately owned is occasionally open to view for parties of visitors.

Continue your walk by taking the footpath marked "Severn Way" to the right of the lichgate of the graveyard ahead of you. Keep the graveyard on your left and at the end of the first field cross the stile ahead of you, turn left, following the yellow arrow sign.

Keep the hedge on your left and cross another stile to emerge onto a metalled road. Here you need to make another choice. A very short walk down the road to your right, is the old "Manor House" which is worth detouring to but your route lies to your left. If you visit the manor you will see from the road a beautiful, black and white, "E" shaped, timber framed building, erected in 1460. Inside this period, family home are extensively carved ceiling beams.

Go back to the stile and walk away from the manor for 10 yards then turn right on a well signed footpath, through a private garden keeping the hedge on your right and over another stile into a field.

Ignore the well marked path on your left and go straight across the field towards the metal, five bar gate in the far right-hand corner of the field. Here the footpath divides.

Take the one that goes off, at an angle, to the left across the orchard towards a house. Go through a wooden gate, following a yellow arrow and cross the private drive. Go through another gate and cross this field at right angles.

A final pair of stiles are found in the corner of the field, which you cross to again go through a private garden and emerge on the village road. The "Queen's Arms'" and your car are now a short walk off to your left.

WALK 3

Bibury to Coneygar

Distance: 4 1/2 miles

Allow: 2 1/2 hours

"An adventurous walk centred on one of the area's prettiest and most popular villages, Bibury. The walk takes in some quite breathtaking scenery along the River Coln before climbing high above the village through woodland and wind blown fields. All of this with a lovely old Cotswold pub to celebrate in near to the finish."

Park near the bridge over the River Coln in the centre of Bibury, as the walk starts and ends opposite the "Swan Hotel".

This walk has eating and drinking places at the beginning and again at the end. The "Swan Hotel" is a very popular, up market hotel offering a wide range of both alcoholic and non-alcoholic drinks as well as snacks and full meals. At the other end of the spectrum you will find a "fast food" or ice cream van parked near to the bridge. Or for something in between there is the quaint little "Jenny Wren" tea rooms just a short walk from the start.

Set off from the bridge, following the B4425 road towards Burford, keeping the River Coln on your right.

This first short section is the main tourist mecca, where on almost 365 days of the year you will find visitors captivated by the sight of enormous trout, in the river below competing for tit bits alongside ducks, swans, moorhens and coots.

Across the river is "Rack Island" and the world famous Arlington Row, a scene often seen on calendars and chocolate boxes. Now owned and maintained by "The National Trust", these tiny cottages were built in the 14th Century as a wool store and were later converted into houses for weavers, whose job it was to wash out sheep fleeces and hang them out to dry, on the island.

There is a mini circular walk around the island which you may wish to do on your return.

Pass Arlington Row and continue along the B4425 until it sweeps out of the village and away to your left. Ahead of you is a "no entry" road. Leave the main road and walk straight ahead into the "no entry" road and head for the church, still keeping the river on your right.

The church is St.Mary's and is well worth a visit before pressing on. It is a peaceful oasis in this busy village. Surrounded on all sides by lawns and ancient tombstones, the church offers sanctuary on a hot day and has some most interesting features. It dates back to Anglo-Saxon times but was extensively added to by the Normans and feels very different to other Cotswold churches.

From the church continue up the road passing the primary school on your right. Along here the tiny cottages seem to crowd in on you from both sides as you climb the gentle slope. Now pass the telephone kiosk on your left.

At the "T" junction turn right and pass "Corner Cottage" on your right. After a few yards the B4425 sweeps left for Burford and you need to follow the minor road towards Coln St.Aldwyns. After a further 40 yards turn right down a tarmac drive following a "bridle way" sign towards a fine manor house and a large stone mill wheel. On your right is the church.

At the bottom of this slope, off to your right, is the "Bibury Court Hotel" which looks truly wonderful in this gem of a location. Running alongside it is the Coln which has now become quite a substantial river being some 20 to 25 feet in width, having started its life as a spring near Cleeve Common.

This section is easy walking as you cross the river and follow the track, first to the right and then to the left between an ancient mill building and a grand old house with neat terraced gardens.

Climb the slope and when the track divides ignore the footpath to the right and continue straight ahead on the "bridle way". Along here you are treated to unrivalled views of the Coln and back over your left shoulder a modern manor house with commanding views of the lush valley basin and surrounding woodlands. This is sheep and pheasant country and both can often be seen here in large numbers.

After 200 yards ignore the track going off to your right and continue straight ahead up the slope. Here is a good opportunity to catch your breath and look back on a truly unforgettable view of the river, valley and manor house.

At the top of the slope the track becomes a muddy path which sweeps off left and you continue to follow it, still with the river on your left. Ignore any paths going off to your right. You have a wood and a dry stone wall on your left for the next part of the journey.

When the path peters out go through a wooden gate and continue in the same line, with the wall still on your left. At the end of this field the path closes in on you as you go straight on and start to drop down a steep slope, passing through a wooden gate.

Remember this is a well used "bridle way" so if the weather has been wet this path can become very muddy and slippery. At the bottom of the slope go through the gate and cross the brook.

Now cross the field diagonally left and make for a metal gate. The walking is once again very flat and easy as you follow the line of the river, which at this point seems to be an integral part of the field, with no banks to speak of. It is very tranquil and an ideal spot to just stop and spend a little time in.

Go through the metal gate and keep the wood on your right. Very soon you come to a second metal gate. Do not go through it but leave the path and turn sharp right to go up a steep slope along the edge of the wood.

At the top of this short, steep slope when the ground flattens out, ignore the track going off to the right and continue straight ahead, leaving the wood behind you. The walking again becomes very easy.

The track eventually emerges between two houses onto a busy country road. This is Coneygar. Here you turn right and walk down the road, taking great care. After about 120 yards turn right onto a well used track where again the walking is easy as you start to drop down hill. There are good views in all directions.

Looking off to your right you will see the "Downs" which were once used as a racecourse. Bibury was the headquarters for one of the oldest racing clubs in the country in the 1600's and attracted vast crowds of racegoers including the reigning monarch, Charles II.

Pass through a metal gate and continue downhill through lush, green pastures which are very pretty and very English. There is a fine view of a copse ahead of you which you are now heading for.

At the bottom of the slope go through another gate, over a brook and keeping the copse on your left, begin to climb the slope. This track can get very muddy when the weather has been wet. Ignore any tracks going off to your right and stay on the track for about a mile. The next part is difficult to follow.

Having eventually passed a dry stone wall going off to your right continue straight on for 100 yards until you see houses both in front of you and to your right.

The track now divides and you will see a metal gate and a crude home made sign on your left, showing the tracks for Ready Token, Coln St.Aldwyns and Bibury. Here you turn right on a grassy track, in the middle of the field and have on your left a thin line of trees. Off to your left is a row of houses in Bibury village. This is again easy walking.

You are now heading for a house with two tall chimneys and pass under electricity cables. Just before the house the path divides in various directions. Here turn left and cross a large stone stile.

The path drops down hill towards the village and you have a dry stone wall on your right. At the bottom of this slope, cross a stile and the path pops out onto the main village road.

On your right is the 15th Century Inn, the "Catherine Wheel" which offers just about everything for the hungry walker including snacks, a full menu and a wide range of ales. This cosy inn with its massive ship's timbers as beams, stone walls and log fires is full of atmosphere that makes the walker want to linger. In good weather a lovely garden offers a cool place to rest a while before moving on. It even advertises itself as "The happiest pub in the Cotswolds".

From the pub cross over to the footpath to follow the main road down hill. On your left is the Village Stores and Post Office and a few yards further on "Arlington Mill" which is now a museum. Alongside the mill is the famous trout farm whose many escapees have found refuge in the Coln.

You are now back at your car having completed the circular walk and once again have the opportunity to visit the "Swan Hotel" or the nearby tea rooms.

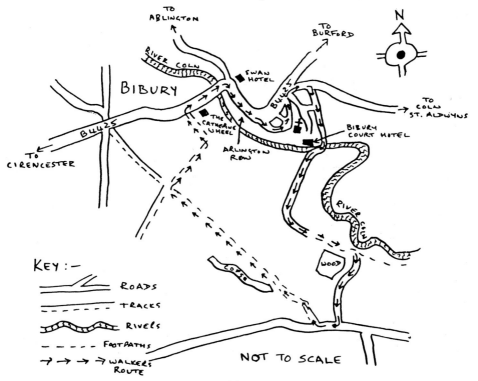

WALK 4

Bourton-on-the-Water via the lakes

Distance: 3 miles

Allow: 2 hours

"An easy stroll in the heart of the country with the added attractions of lakes and birds with the convenience of shops, pubs and tea shops. A truly unique view of a village that has so much to offer."

Park your car in the spacious council car park next to Birdland on Rissington Road and begin your walk by turning right out of the car park and heading out of the village. Take the first turning to your right which is only marked as a "no through road" with a second sign which reads "No access to Birdland".

This is easy walking as you follow the narrow road out of the built up area to cross the pretty, fast flowing River Windrush which will accompany you for much of the walk. Look out for the spectacular explosion of colour of the kingfishers who are at home along this stretch of river and are a regular sight.

There are fine views all around this peaceful farmland and you have animals for company. On the ridge to your left is Little Rissington and its famous airfield which has seen so much action over the years. This was home to the legendary squadron "The Red Arrows", for many years and has as a memorial to them a fine stained glass window of one of their jets in the village church.

To your right is the village of Clapton on the Hill.

As you pass Marshmouth Farm further on your right, take time to study the fingerpost on your left which indicates the mileage in "as the crow flies" miles and endorses the message with two fine model crows, keeping guard over the sign.

When the road sweeps right, leave it and continue straight ahead on a "bridle way". At the first house with its own old fashioned telephone kiosk turn left on the yellow arrowed path which continues as a broad track.

Go over a stile and when the track sweeps right, leave it and go straight on over another stile and into a field, keeping the fence on your left. You now have a brook joining you on your left as you continue ahead over two further stiles.

Here you once again meet the fast flowing Windrush and cross it over two wooden bridges. Take a break at this point to stop and admire the watery view below you. It is here that the River Windrush merges with its smaller brothers, the Eye and the Dickler, which had in turn joined forces a mile away.

The area is rich in wildlife and it is quite common to see large trout, coots, geese, grebes, ducks, herons and even black swans. Life is as it ought to be here and you should not hurry to leave it behind.

Cross one more stile and enter the lake area which was formally two gravel pits and is quite breathtaking. When the footpath divides at this point take the one to your left. You now have the Windrush on your left and the first of the two lakes on your right.

Mid-way along the second lake follow the yellow arrowed path off to your left to re-cross the river over a narrow bridge. Cross a stile and turn right and after 10 yards enter a little copse on your right via another stile. Now follow the footpath left as it threads its way through the

12

copse.

At the end of this path, as it pops out from the copse, go to your right over a wide wooden bridge to re-cross the Windrush and follow the track straight ahead towards the main road. As the track sweeps left, the last short section is not a right of way, so enter the field on your right via a stile and keep straight ahead, parallel with the track.

You are now back on Rissington Road and here you walk to your right for some 15 yards before crossing the road and entering a field on your left, over a stile and following a "footpath" arrow.

Cross the field with houses on your left and another gravel lake on your right. These lakes are fished by "Moreton Angling Club" and make a splendid splash of colour, dotted as they are with an abundance of wildlife including ducks and grebes.

Cross another stile and a small bridge and continue straight ahead on a well defined track. Here you pass behind a long row of houses to emerge onto a much broader track and a division of paths. Take the path off to your left.

Stay on this track for about a quarter of a mile and as soon as you pass a large, stone wall on your left and with allotments on your right, look out for a footpath slightly below you on the left. Take this well used path as it doubles back on you through some trees and then goes around to the right.

The track soon merges with the driveway to a house where you turn right and walk down the drive. Your journey is now at an end as you once again cross Rissington Road to the car park on your left and your car.

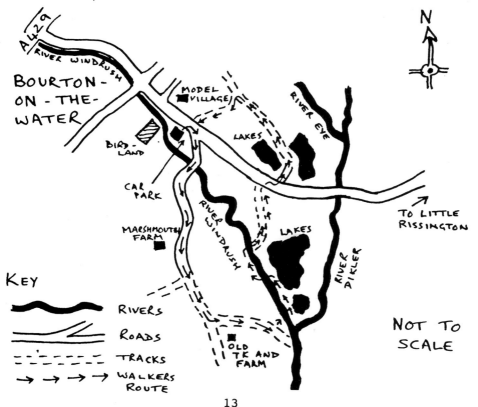

WALK 5

Coln St. Aldwyns to Coneygar

Distance: 4 miles

Allow: 2 hours

"A splendid stroll through open farmland, beginning and ending in the pretty Cotswold village of Coln St.Aldwyns. The walk offers a varied landscape never far from a lovely river and a pub to remember long after the adventure - a day you will not forget in a hurry."

The walk starts at the lovely old Norman church dedicated to St.John the Baptist in the centre of Coln St.Aldwyns. Park the car well off the village roads, taking the opportunity to visit the church either now or on your return.

From the church gates walk down into the village and turn left. Very soon you pass some fine old cottages on your right which are built of local stone and timber from the nearby Williamstrip House estate, the home of Earl St.Aldwyns.

Follow the road as it sweeps to the right into the centre of the village and turn right, following the signs for Quennington and Fairford. This is a nice place to just stop and look around at some fine stone buildings and a lovely old tree right in the centre of the village. If you time your walk to coincide with the opening hours of the village shop you can stock up on a range of food and drinks for the walk ahead.

You are now going to walk down the road for a short way and need to cross over and use the safety of the footpath as the road gets quite busy although it is only a minor country road. As you drop down the village you pass the "New Inn" on your left. This is a "free house", offering a fine selection of meals and snacks and a wide range of ales. You can choose to visit it either now or on your return.

Carry on down the road and very soon you pass a lovely old mill on your right and a pretty water garden on the left and it is here that you also get your first view of the fast flowing, clear waters of the River Coln.

Continue down the road for a further 400 yards. Already the views are quite idyllic, with Cotswold stone cottages set alongside a watery meadow. It is quite common to see a wide variety of wildlife including swans, ducks, coots, moorhen and Canada geese contentedly living out their lives in this green Gloucestershire sanctuary.

Cross over the little river bridge and immediately turn right into the entrance to a cottage. Go through a second wooden gate and here the path divides. Leave the riverside and take the "bridle way" that goes off up the field at a left angle, towards the trees.

Here again you get a fine view of the twisting path of the River Coln and the valley below; this is sheep country and the scene laid out below you is very English. Climb to the top of the slope, passing through an avenue of trees and now the walking becomes very easy. Take time at the top to catch your breath and look back at the village. The views on this walk get better and better.

Keep the dry stone wall on your left and you eventually go through a metal gate and the footpath continues straight ahead towards a farm in the distance with a large grey barn. Walk towards the farm to go through a gap in the wall and continue straight ahead towards some cottages.

Go through a metal gate to pass the two cottages on your right and then the grey barns on

14

your left. Follow the dry stone wall and go through a metal gate. Here the footpath divides. Follow the painted signs straight ahead towards a cottage called "Coneygar Lodge".

Just before the Lodge, leave the field through a gate on your left. Here you join a minor country road which you follow to your right. Take care for although this is a minor road it can get very busy. Pass the Lodge and turn right on a well used track that runs between the two buildings.

The track is broad and flat and leads you back towards the River Coln. After 400 yards the track divides; continue straight ahead keeping the hedge on your right and the wood on your left as you begin to drop steeply down hill. Half way down the hill you are once again treated to a fine view of the snaking River Coln and the green valley that will accompany you home.

When the track ends turn right, go through a metal gate and continue straight ahead, keeping the river on your left. This is a most pleasant section of the walk which should not be hurried for you could almost be walking in a "Constable" painting. At the end of this field go through another metal gate and keep straight on.

After two more fields you come to an old, green footpath sign and turn right to walk away from the river towards the wood in the far distance. It is here that you cross the ancient path of the former Roman road, Akeman Street. Soon the path sweeps left and you have the pine wood on your right.

At the end of the dry stone wall, go through a gate and continue straight ahead on the path through the middle of the wood. After a short walk go through a second gate and continue ahead across the field, once again having the river for company on your left.

It is time to slow down again and enjoy this last section as you cross the field and retrace your steps back to Coln St.Aldwyns, your awaiting car and a second chance to visit the "New Inn", a pub you will not forget in a hurry.

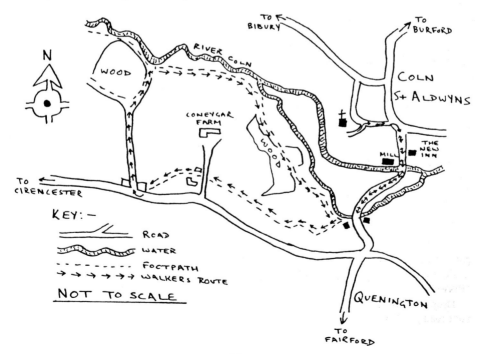

KEY:-

———————— ROAD

〜〜〜〜〜 WATER

- - - - - - - - FOOTPATH

→ → → → → → WALKERS ROUTE

NOT TO SCALE

WALK 6

Cowley to Upper Coberley

Distance: 3 1/2 miles

Allow: 2 hours

"A majestical walk through open fields, offering uninterrupted views of large tracks of Gloucestershire. With a hidden valley and a country pub in the old style, this is a lovely spring and summer walk."

The walk starts from the telephone kiosk in the centre of Cowley outside the manor gates. There are parking spaces here for up to three cars.

Cowley Manor was until recently owned by Gloucestershire County Council and used as a training centre but has now been converted into a community care home.

Within the private grounds of the manor is the village church which is well worth visiting, either now or at the end of this short walk. St.Mary's Church and Cowley village are believed to be the places where Lewis Carroll found the inspiration to write the classic tale of "Alice in Wonderland".

Walk out of the village along the road back towards the main A435 Cheltenham to Cirencester road, keeping the manor grounds on your right. You cross the infant River Churn, beginning its long journey to the distant Thames, and pass through a fine avenue of trees. Here you can see the village of Coberley off to your left.

Cross the main road with great care and enter the country lane opposite and begin to make your way up the gentle slope. The views quickly open up and as you catch your breath you are treated to fine, uninterrupted views back over the Birdlip escarpment and surrounding farms. This is sheep country and you can readily see flocks of them around.

Before long you enter the pretty little hamlet of Upper Coberley with a converted "Dutch" barn on your left and an old farm building on your right. Just before the farm, leave the road and turn right onto a wide, stony track.

You are now walking back on yourself parallel with the road you just left. Unbelievably, the views now extend to take in a Cotswold panorama which is second to none. Cowley lies below you and lush green fields ripple away from you, like a meadowy ocean.

The walking is both firm and easy as limestone turns into tarmac to take you back down the slope towards the A435 below, through "Westbury Farm".

At the main road, again exercise great care as you cross straight over and go down the driveway to a private house (do not worry, this is a "public footpath" and you are not trespassing). There is a post box on your right and the gateway has a gated entrance.

The footpath in fact passes right in front of the house which you pass on your right to once again cross the River Churn. This is a delightful spot.

Now follow the footpath as it climbs away from the river up the steep slope. At the top the path meets a narrow country lane in the heart of the hamlet of Cockleford and here you turn right.

Follow the road back towards Cowley and at the "T" junction, just after a farm called "Pixwold", turn right.

Drop down the slope with care as this is a busy road and your way back takes you left at the next road junction.

16

However, about 100 yards further down the slope, on the right is the delightfully authentic Cotswold pub, the "Green Dragon". This is a "free house" offering a wide choice of ales and an extensive menu and is well worth a visit.

Now take the narrow country lane back to Cowley. On your right you pass "Deerpark" the county's Girl Guide Headquarters and Training Centre and just after you get a fabulous side on view of Cowley Manor itself. Looking out over its well kept lawns you can see the water garden and terraces and easily imagine the opulent history of this once great house.

At the next "T" junction turn right and walk back to your car to end a lovely, historic and charming walk.

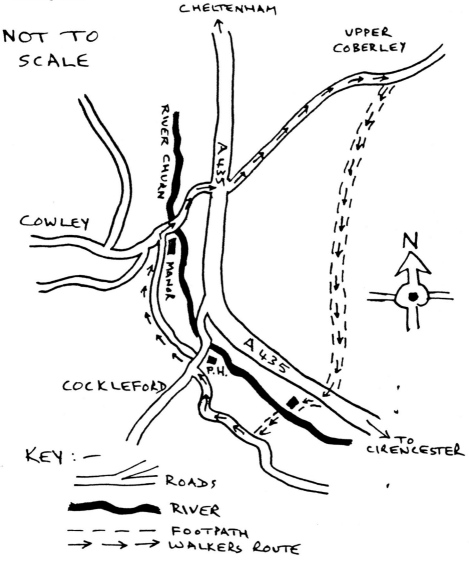

WALK 7

Elkstone to Cockleford

Distance: 4 miles
Allow: 2 hours

"A testing walk through fields and woods, offering a varied landscape and fine views. This circular stroll takes in a country pub half way round, and a chance to rest before the hilly finish."

The walk begins in the grounds of the village church at Elkstone.

This is St. John's and is well worth visiting if only for the unique colours radiating throughout the interior of the church from a variety of stained glass windows. The Chancel is particularly beautiful, bathed in golden refracted light which gives it a feeling of perpetual sunshine.

Go around to the back of the church and leave the grounds through a small gate with an old street light on your right. Continue straight ahead and after 15 yards cross a stile, following the yellow arrowed signs.

Now keep the metal fence on your right as you cross the field. Go over a large stone stile and continue ahead with a dry stone wall on your right, to cross another wooden stile.

You now have a wooden fence on your right before once again crossing a stile to pass between the houses. Cross a stone stile and follow the path as it first goes left and then right, at the bottom of a private garden. Pass through a metal gate to emerge on a narrow country lane; here you turn left.

Follow the road to a crossroads and go straight over to pass a telephone kiosk on your left. You are on the road to Brimpsfield and Birdlip.

Very soon the road sweeps right and you follow it for a short distance to a "T" junction. Here you leave the road and walk straight ahead, across the field, following a footpath sign towards the woods in the distance.

At this point you are very high and have almost unrestricted views in all directions. To the right is Cleeve Common, to the left Birdlip and back over your left shoulder the Stroud valley.

When the footpath arrives at the edge of the wood you meet an old farm gate. Below you, through a gap in the trees, is the magnificent sight of Cowley Manor and its neat little village. Climb the gate and head downhill in a line with the manor house.

As you drop down, pass the gamekeeper's hut on your left, ignore the tracks going off to your right and left and continue straight ahead, down the steep slope.

At the bottom of the hill you get into thick woodland and a wide variety of trees. The going here can be a little muddy so take your time to reach the valley basin

Here the path divides. Ignore the yellow arrowed path on your right which rises steeply and also the track going off to your left.

Take the second path on your right, marked with a blue arrow, to walk through the wood, with a brook on your left for company. At the wood's end the path divides and you go straight ahead, following the blue "bridle way" arrows, keeping the hedge on your left.

At the end of this field the path comes out onto a minor country road. Your way goes off to the right. However 100 yards down to your left is the charming Cotswold pub, the "Green Dragon" which is worth detouring to. It's a "free house" and offers an extensive range of good food and ales.

Now, to complete your journey, walk back up the road and take the first turning left, marked "Cockleford - no through road".

You are now walking parallel with the busy A435 Cheltenham to Cirencester road, but for all that it could be a million miles away as you feel as if you are deep in the heart of the country.

Follow the lane for about a quarter of a mile, pass "The Cottage" and drop down into a dip. Climb back up the gentle slope and opposite the next cottages on your left is a track going off to your right, marked as a "public path". Take this track.

You now start on a steep climb, marked every now and again with orange arrowed markers.

As you climb, fabulous views begin to open up in all directions. The fields undulate like rolling waves making their way to the little villages of Cowley, Cockleford, Coberley and Colesbourne.

As the path finally flattens out you arrive at a small wooded copse where you go through a metal gate. Continue on the track with the wood on your left.

After a further 300 yards the track emerges onto a minor country road and here you turn right.

Now take care. There are two "public paths" going off to your left. Ignore the first one and walk down the road for about 20 yards. Pass a converted barn and take the path just after it, on your left. You now have the converted barn, "Sparrowthorn", on your left.

The walking again is very easy and the views unrestricted. Ahead and to your left is the line of the Roman road, Ermin Street.

Soon the path divides in four directions. Ignore the tracks going off left and right and continue straight ahead, down into Elkstone village.

When the track meets the village road, turn left and follow the road for a short distance as it makes its way around the village and back to the church.

WALK 8

Frampton on Severn to Church End

Distance: 3 miles

Allow: 1 1/2 hours

"A flat stroll through open farmland, beginning and ending in one of Gloucestershire's prettiest villages. With a varied landscape and two pubs for a rest, this is a very different walk."

The walk starts and ends in the little village car park, off the famous "Rosamund's Green" at Frampton-on-Severn, between the Post Office and the "Bell Inn".

Frampton's green is one of England's largest, surrounded by an architectural mixture of old and new buildings, ranging from Georgian and half-timbered houses to neat modern semis and detached homes.

Henry II's mistress, Jane Clifford, so called "Fair Rosamund", was born here and it is after her that the green takes its name. Frampton and its green are truly old places and the green even sports a cricket pitch, conveniently situated outside the "Bell".

The pub itself is a Whitbread pub, offering a wide range of beers and food and is well worth visiting either now or on your return.

To begin the walk, cross the green, with the pub on your left, turn right into Bridge Road and walk in the direction of Gloucester. You now have to walk on the road. Take great care as this is a very busy road and carries lots of traffic.

After 200 yards, leave the road and enter the grounds of "Frampton Court". Here are a magnificent pair of wrought iron gates and to the left of them a "kissing gate". Go through this gate into the grounds and follow the yellow arrow marker straight ahead, keeping the lake on your left.

The Court itself is off to your right. It was built in the Palladian style in the 1730's for a Bristol customs official, Richard Clutterbuck, and is a most imposing building.

Already you are right in the heart of the country and the busy road at the beginning of the walk seems a million miles away.

The lake is covered with a variety of wildlife, each adding a splash of colour to the grey water. Little islands are home to ducks, moorhens, coots, swans and any number of Canada geese. If you look above the water line into the islands' trees, cormorants can often be seen preening themselves and drying their wings in the sun, readying themselves for their return to the watery hunting grounds.

As the lake ends, veer slightly right towards a pair of semi-detached cottages. To the left of them is a stile, cross it and the little lane and re-enter the fields over a second stile.

Now cross the field by walking diagonally left, keeping a small cottage to your left, heading for a pair of metal gates and a wooded copse. Just to the right of the gates is another stile and a footpath sign. Cross the stile and continue straight ahead.

After about 20 yards there is a stile on your left. Ignore this stile and begin to veer off at a slight right angle towards a large converted barn. If you feel at all lost, look out for the church tower in the distance, as you should be walking in a direct line towards it.

This is flat country and the walking is easy. It is also sailing and horse riding country. All around are grazing horses and off to your left the masts of sailing boats on yet another lake.

Cross another stile and small track and then keep walking straight ahead over a series of stiles.

The barn you saw is now clearly visible and you will see that it has in fact been converted into the club house for Frampton-on-Severn's Sailing Club.

Having passed the club house, go over one more stile into a field and turn left. Cross the field, keeping a fence on your left and at the end of the field cross yet another stile. You are now walking along a narrow lane with the sailing lake on your left and a small, private lake on your right.

At the end of the lane you emerge onto a road; now keep straight on with the houses on your right. The lane has now become a wide track.

After about 100 yards and just after the last house, turn right and follow the yellow arrow sign over a stile. You still have the houses on your right.

This narrow lane soon peters out and as you cross another stile, exercise great care as you emerge right onto a country road. Here go slightly left and follow the road towards the church. This is Church End and it is here that you pass a fine old 15th Century barn.

You will come back here to visit the church but for now stay on the road as it sweeps off left and down to the canal.

The road ends at the canal bridge and from here you are treated to magnificent views out across the Severn estuary and deep into the Forest of Dean.

Do not cross the canal bridge but turn sharp right onto the bank of the Gloucester to Sharpness Canal and pass the lock-keeper's box on your right.

If you are very lucky you may be treated to the sight of a boat making its way to or from Gloucester Docks. The canal was built to take sea-going vessels into the heart of the city and is still regularly used for this purpose.

Follow the towpath for about 25 yards and then go off to your right, to cross a brook over a small concrete bridge. Now ignore the path to your left and walk straight ahead across the field, in the direction of a stone cross.

Cross a stile and turn left to visit St.Mary's Church. Quite often the door to the church is locked but the key is available from nearby, Church House.

From the church gate walk towards the canal, keeping the church on your right and cross a stile. Now go off to the right again, keeping the churchyard on your right.

As you make your way back towards the village you pass through an ancient avenue of trees and a lych-gate before re-joining the road. Now keep straight ahead to pass through the village.

Here is a second pub, the "Three Horseshoes", which is a cosy pub offering good food and ales and a chance to play traditional pub games.

All around you is a true mixture of architectural styles with Tudor cottages happily rubbing shoulders with "Dutch" style houses and modern homes.

Keep the houses on your left and the green on your right for a further quarter of a mile, back to your car and another chance to visit the "Bell Inn".

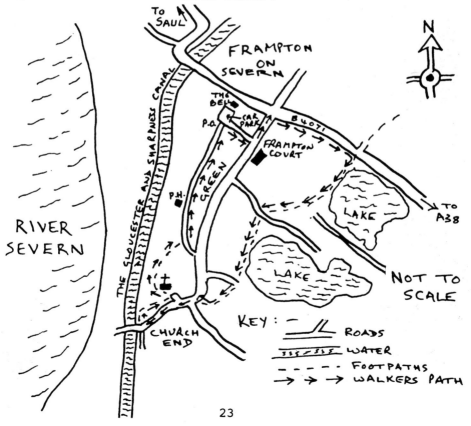

WALK 9

Guiting Power to Hawling Lodge

Distance: 4 miles
Allow: 2 hours

"A triangular walk based around one of the Cotswolds' finest villages, offering stops at two pubs, a Post Office and a bakery and general store. A very easy walk when the weather is good."

The walk starts at the stone cross in the centre of Guiting Power yet a good place to park your car is in the nearby carpark of the village hall, close to the church. This is a "trust" carpark and money you donate goes to a good, local cause. Park here and make your way back to the cross to savour the scene of this lovely village before you set off on your journey.

Guiting Power is a village which shouts "Cotswolds". The golden coloured limestone cottages make a marvellous border to the splendid sloping green and stone cross. If the sun is shining then no photographer could move on without first capturing this scene for posterity.

From the cross you can see "Watsons Bakery" which offers fresh bread and a wide selection of groceries. Opposite is the Post Office and its supply of provisions and at each end of the village is a pub. Both offer,"real ales" and excellent meals. These are the Donnington pub the "Farmers Arms" and a "free house" called "Ye Olde Inne".

Leave the green and turn right at the bakery to walk out of the village on a metalled road which soon sweeps round to the right in front of the recently closed school building. Walk out of the village staying on the road as it begins to taper down into a single track. You are on public roads for a lot of the walk and need to be conscious of that fact. Although they are quiet by town standards they are, nevertheless, in regular use.

Already fine views open up to your left, back across the village with its handsome Norman church and on out towards Naunton. There are several well known walks that converge in Guiting Power, including the "Wardens' Way", the "Windrush Way" and my own walk, the "Donnington Way".

Soon the hedgerows disappear and you are walking in open country with panoramic views. After half a mile, at a "Y" junction, continue straight on. To your left are some fine farm houses, a lake and a splendid old house. From here it is tempting to stop and stare but be patient for you will return, close to these properties and see them in all their splendour.

Pass "Hawling Lodge Cottages" on your right and after a few yards you meet signs for the "Windrush Way" on your left. Take this path by turning back on yourself and entering the field, through a five bar gate, and walk down into the valley basin.

Here you meet a fast flowing brook, which began life just a mile away at Hawling. Keep it on your right for a few yards before carefully crossing it. Now keep it on your left until the " bridle way" begins to climb away from it, following the line of the overhead electricity cables.

You now have the most glorious views of the house on your left with its neatly walled gardens, pond and lawns. Continue across the field until, after a stile you join the driveway to the house and follow the direction arrow that takes you straight on, up the drive. When you again meet the road, turn right and follow it as it climbs uphill.

At the top the minor road meets the busy B4068 and here you pass the building which was once the popular" Foxhill Inn", now closed.

From the pub, do not enter the "B" road but take the first turning down to your left, towards

Guiting Power and follow the road carefully down hill. This too can be busy at times so exercise caution.

The road sweeps right and then left. In front of you are fabulous views out into the country and below you and slightly to your left is Guiting Power, looking for all the world like the famous model village at Bourton-on-the-Water.

When you arrive at a "T" junction on your right pointing the way to Naunton, turn left onto a well marked and well used footpath. Cross the field and once again pick up the yellow arrows as they take you down hill on series of wooden steps into the "Guiting Power Nature Reserve". Go over the little bridge, cross a stile and walk up a small slope to continue straight ahead.

After crossing this field there is another wooden stile. Now you pass alongside St.Michael's Church and over one last stile to walk up the narrow metalled lane and back to your car.

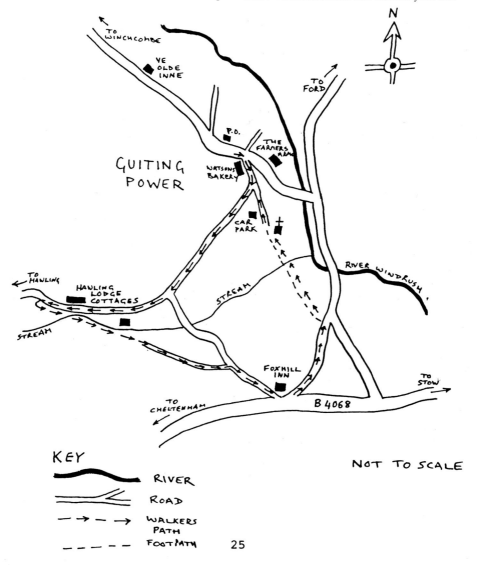

KEY

NOT TO SCALE

—— RIVER

—— ROAD

— → — → WALKERS PATH

— — — — FOOTPATH

25

WALK 10

Lechlade to St.John's Lock

Distance: 3 miles
Allow: 1 1/2 hours

"A flat stroll through a lovely old Cotswold town and an unusual chance to follow England's premier river as it begins its long journey from Gloucestershire to the capital and beyond. A very different walk with some fine old pubs and tea rooms on the way".

The walk begins outside the County Library in the centre of Lechlade where you can park your car close to the church of St.Lawrence. The church is well worth visiting now or on your return.

Building of the church began in 1470 on the site of a previous church. In many respects it has a mini cathedral feel inside and is described as being one of the six finest churches in Gloucestershire.

Leaving the church behind you, walk out of the town on the A417 road towards Fairford, passing the Police Station on your left. Lechlade is a lovely old Cotswold market town and boasts many pubs and tea shops around the centre, all of which can be visited now or on your return. There are also several mini supermarkets where you can stock up on provisions for the journey.

Take time to browse in the shops as you walk out of town. They range from food shops to any number of antique shops and also include the unusual feature of an all year Christmas gift shop.

After about 400 yards from the shops on the A417, at the end of a layby, leave the road and take a footpath to your left which is well signed and crosses over a concrete stile into the fields. You have an old fence and stream on your right at this point.

The path now crosses several meadows over a series of wooden stiles and small bridges. The walking is flat and easy and the countryside is green and lush. Some of the stiles are old and worn and should be crossed with care. Off to the left are the first tantalizing views of the River Thames or Isis with its colourful pleasure crafts.

Lechlade is the end of the navigable section of the river and the turning point for the many crafts that make the long journey from the capital.

At the end of this field section go over a stile and turn left onto a metalled road and after 10 yards turn left again onto a well made track which is marked by a footpath sign. Cross over a cattle grid and from this point look ahead and slightly left, here you will see a wooden bridge that will shortly take you over the river.

Just before a second cattle grid leave the track and go down a little narrow path to your left, having some very old trees on your left and make your way down to the river, keeping it on your right. Look over your right shoulder here and you will see the remains of a roundhouse which indicates the point where the Thames & Severn Canal once joined the river. The canal opened in 1789 and was abandoned in 1927. Also at this point the River Coln flows into the Thames to end its journey from the base of Cleeve Common.

Follow the path across the river bridge and onto the far bank, turn left and keep the river on your left. You now keep the river on your left for a considerable part of the journey. The walking continues to be flat and easy and there is a wide variety of wildlife using the river as you pass by. This is a very pretty section and should not be hurried.

Soon you pass a boatyard on your left and get a tantalizing view of St.Lawrence's church spire, your starting point on the walk. Here you go under "Halfpenny Pike Bridge". The bridge dates back to 1792 when it was constructed as a toll bridge to replace the old Tidford Ferry which had been used for years to cross the river.

Continue to follow the river, enjoying the fine views on offer to your left of the properties in the main street and the church still dominating the skyline.

At the end of the river section you walk alongside St.John's Lock between the lock and keeper's house. Here too is a place to linger a while. Watching the antics of some of the holiday boatmen can be quite an amusing aside.

On the Lock is a lifesize statue of "Father Thames" keeping a weather eye on the river

activities. The statue was commissioned in 1854 for The Crystal Palace and marked the head of the Thames at Trewsbury Mead until 1974 when it was moved to St.John's Lock.

Walk past the lock, leave the river just before the bridge and follow the steps up to the A417 road where you turn left. Now cross the road bridge with great care as this is a well used road. It is well worth stopping as you cross the bridge to look back to your left and admire the view of the river, lock and meadows.

On your right is the famous "Trout Inn", a pub offering a fine selection of snacks and meals along with a wide range of beers, including "real ales". The riverside garden attached to the inn is a truly magical place to stop for a while. Here you can play or watch traditional games being played such as boules and "Aunt Sally" and once again get a fabulous view of the Thames.

Follow the A417 from the pub back into Gloucestershire and just before the county sign turn left on a well used and well made footpath that runs between the hedgerows.

At the end of this avenue cross a stile and continue straight ahead across the field. Leave the field and go straight on into the churchyard which is a pleasant oasis. You are walking in the steps of the classic poet Shelley, on a walk named after the great man. It was here that he got his inspiration for the poem "A summers evening in a churchyard, Lechlade", whilst staying in the nearby "New Inn".

You are now back in the centre of Lechlade which offers you a second chance to celebrate the walk in one of the town's many inns, hotels or tea shops.

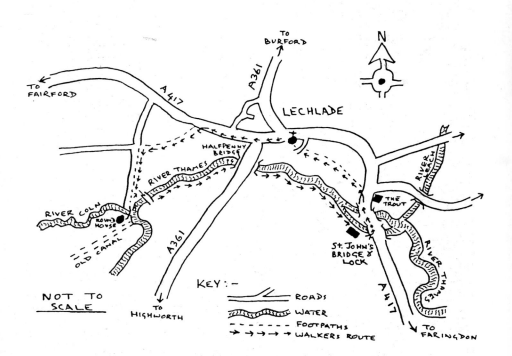

WALK 11

Northleach to Hampnett

Distance: 3 1/2 miles

Allow: 2 hours

"An easy walk over well established paths joining two Cotswold treasures. The walk offers stops at contrasting churches and diversely differing museums. This is a walk with village shops, pubs, hotels and cafés".

Park your car in the market place right in the heart of Northleach where you will find a good selection of shops and pubs to set you on your way and greet you again on your return.

Northleach is a fine old "wool" town which got its name from the mere fact that it was built just north of the River Leach. Built on the wealth of the wool trade it boasts a magnificent 15th Century church which dominates the town centre and is well worth a visit before you set off.

From the market place walk into High Street and turn right at the "Cotswold Stores". Very soon you pass on your left the award winning museum, "Keith Harding's World of Mechanical Music". This features antique clocks, musical boxes, automata and mechanical musical instruments of all kinds and is worth taking time out to visit.

After a further 150 yards turn right into Meadow Lane and walk down the lane into a playing field where you walk left around the tennis courts and then right, keeping the swings on your left. Very soon you will come to a wooden "kissing gate" on your left which you pass through and turn right, following the yellow arrowed sign up a gentle slope.

Take your time climbing the field and while you catch your breath look back at the marvellous view over the town below and its lovely church.

At the top of the field climb a wooden stile and continue to go straight ahead, keeping the dry stone wall on your right. When the field ends the footpath is crossed by a wide track which is a "public path". Here you turn right for an easy stroll with commanding views.

The track eventually crosses a minor metalled road and continues straight ahead towards farm cottages and a large farm barn. Pass between the buildings and stay on the track as it runs between the fields, always heading for the main road ahead.

The track becomes a footpath for the last few yards, ending at a wooden gate which you pass through to cross the busy A429 Foss Way with great care. Continue straight ahead down a minor road indicating the way to Yanworth.

This is easy walking and takes you down to a small reservoir on your right. At the end of the fence turn right, once again on a wide grass track which is a "bridle way". The views remain delightful as you pass through two long fields to once again cross a metalled road, taking care to go straight ahead on a "public path" towards the little hidden village of Hampnett.

Follow the track down hill to the bottom where there is a choice of paths. Your path lies straight ahead through a metal gate on a wide grass track up towards a large country house.

Immediately after passing the house look for a yellow arrowed path on your right which you enter through a metal gate.

Very soon, at the metalled road, turn left and follow the road up into this pretty little village which is the birth place of the River Leach. Take time to call in at St.George's Church which you pass on your left and is a true delight.

Your path now takes you out of the village for 200 yards when you once again leave the road to join a footpath on your right and you go through a wooden "kissing gate", immediately opposite the entrance to "Manor Farm".

Depending upon the time of year, this footpath can be difficult to find so follow the arrow as it indicates the way diagonally across the field to the two tallest trees in the copse ahead. Here is a wooden stile which you cross and follow a yellow arrow sign straight ahead, making for the church tower in the far distance. Cross a second stile and veer slightly right as the arrow indicates.

Follow the path as it crosses the field and goes over the brook. Here turn left and, keeping the brook on your left, make towards the far right hand corner of the field. Climb the stile and turn left to make your way back into Northleach and your car.

If time permits the famous museum, "Cotswold Countryside Collection" is well worth a visit. It is dedicated to all aspects of rural life and social history of the area and is housed in an 18th Century, "House of Correction".

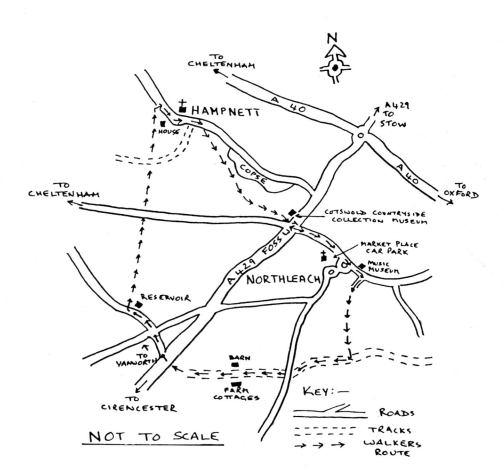

WALK 12

Norton to Wainlode

Distance: 4 miles

Allow: 2 hours

"A classic walk between two pubs, offering some of the finest views in Gloucestershire. An outing in open countryside blessed with an abundance of wildlife. This is a walk that you will long remember."

Park your car in the village of Norton off the A38 Gloucester to Tewkesbury road, close to the "King's Head" public house. The walk starts from the pub, which you may choose to visit now or at the end. The "King's Head" offers a wide range of beers, including "real ales"; and also boasts an extensive menu.

Walk out of the village in the direction of Tewkesbury until you reach a point where the village road almost meets the busy A38. Here you will find a footpath sign directing you off to your left, which you need to follow. At this point you already have fine views off to your right of Leckhampton Hill, Cleeve Common and the Norman church at Prior's Norton.

A short gravelled path takes you down towards a field. Directly in front of you is a stile and yellow arrow sign; do not go over this stile but look carefully for a narrow track just before it, taking you off to the right. This track is not marked and is easily missed.

You now have a small ditch on your left as you weave your way through a small wooded area. Before long you cross a stone bridge, turn right and cross a stile. The field that you are now in can get quite wet at times so make sure that you are wearing appropriate footwear. Follow the yellow arrow marker across this field at a slight left angle.

The footpath takes you to the far left hand corner of the field where you cross a concrete bridge and turn left. Off to your right is a fine view of Bredon Hill and in the foreground another Norman church in the tiny hamlet of The Leigh. To your left lie the Malvern Hills, looking quite glorious from this angle.

Cross over a broken stile in the left hand corner of this field and head straight on. Just before the end of this field cross over another concrete bridge on your left and go through a metal gate.

After a few yards there is a second metal gate. Turn right just in front of it onto a footpath marked with a yellow arrow and black dot. You now have a hedge on your left and you are walking up a slight slope. The way so far has been flat and easy. Take a few seconds at this point to catch your breath and admire the views all around you as you stand in this natural basin.

At the end of this field, in the left hand corner, go over a wooden stile, where your path meets a broad dirt track. Here turn to your right and drop down the slope of the track, following a yellow arrow sign.

At the bottom go over another stile and stay close to the overgrown brook on your left - this field can also get very wet. Just before this field ends there is a wide track going off to your left; walk on for two yards and cross a wooden stile on your left. Now turn sharp right and keep the hedge on your right.

At the end of this field the path sweeps left and after 10 yards goes right; you are still following a yellow arrow mark and have the hedge still on your right.

When the field ends cross over another wooden stile into a caravan park and walk off at a slight left angle. Leave the park and follow the track; you are now in Wainlode and the "Red

Lion" public house is on your left.

The view from here is truly magnificent, with the high banks of the Severn off to your left and the river itself snaking its wide passage in front of you. This is your chance to visit the "Red Lion" and sample a wide range of drinks and food or, if you have come prepared, a place to enjoy a picnic.

To complete your journey walk back up the road with the pub on your left. After 20 yards take the footpath into the first field on your right and follow a yellow sign with a blue dot on it. You are now following the "Severn Way" path.

At the top of the slope again take time to catch your breath and look back at the fabulous views of the Malverns to your left and the River Severn on its journey from Tewkesbury. Go over a wooden stile and walk straight ahead, keeping the hedge on your right.

At the end of this field cross another wooden stile and turn left. After 10 yards you have another stile on your right going off into the wood. Do not go over this stile but walk straight ahead up the steep slope of the field, keeping the wood and hedge on your right.

At the top of the slope go through a metal gate and again keep the wood on your right as you pass through a field used as an equestrian cross country course. This is Norton Hill.

Pass a large "Dutch" barn on your right and walk straight ahead for about 400 yards until you come to a "trig point" on your left. Here the path divides and you need to turn back on yourself to the left to follow a yellow arrow mark. There are four trees on your right as a marker.

SEVERN WAY
PATH

You now start to drop downhill and cross a wooden stile. Drop down a steep slope heading to the left of an equestrian water jump. At the bottom turn sharp right and go over a wooden bridge. Here you turn left and keep the hedge on your left.

At the bottom of this field turn left and after 20 yards turn right over a stile and a little wooden bridge. Now keep the hedge and fence on your left as you drop down this field crossing two wooden stiles as you go. You now have some houses on your left.

Soon you turn left and cross another stile to join a narrow farm track. Follow the orange arrow sign to the left, keeping "Yew Tree Farm" on your right. Walk down the road into the hamlet of Bishop's Norton. Take care along here as although this is only a minor road it is quite well used.

After 200 yards you come to the heart of the village and walk over a small green, keeping an interesting pond, island and thatched cottage on your left. Here is an insight into life as it must have been years ago.

Turn right at the road to pass the old Wesleyan Chapel on your right. Stay on the footpath for about half a mile until you come to a "T" junction. Turn left and follow the village road back down to the "King's Head" and your car.

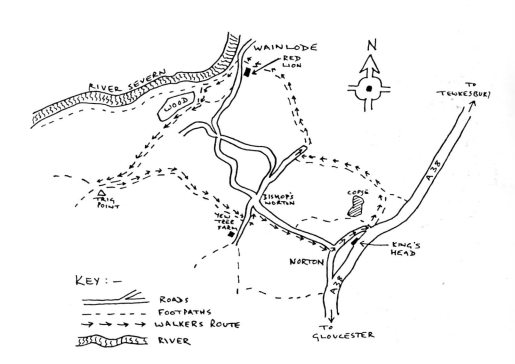

KEY : —

——— ROADS
— — — — — FOOTPATHS
→ → → → WALKERS ROUTE
〰〰〰 RIVER

WALK 13

Pegglesworth to Charlton Kings

Distance: 4 miles
Allow: 2 hours

"A challenging woodland walk offering outstanding views from this Cotswold escarpment to the Forest of Dean and far beyond. An easy stroll down to a comfortable pub and a hilly climb back to the car."

Pegglesworth is an area on the A436 Gloucester to Stow-on-the-Wold road mid-way between Seven Springs and Andoversford. The walk starts from the layby opposite "Pegglesworth House" over a stile that takes you into "Lineover Wood". Parking is limited in the layby and you may be forced to use the large layby some 200 yards away and walk back to the wood. Parts of the walk can get quite muddy so come prepared with appropriate footwear. "Lineover" after which the wood is named means "lime bank" in Anglo Saxon. The wood is 111 acres in size and was first recorded around 800 A.D.

Having crossed the stile and entered the wood the path immediately divides and you need to take the path going off to your left. You are now walking parallel with the "A" road through an avenue of trees on a well used path along the top of the ridge.

Before long some fine views of Cheltenham open up to your right and already you can clearly see Cleeve Common and, in the distance, the Malvern Hills.

At the end of the path drop down slightly to your right and cross a stile then turn right and cross a second stile. Here the yellow arrow signs indicate another divide in the path and you take the left hand track.

Follow the path as it winds its way through the trees. Take care as it becomes narrow in places. Eventually the path emerges into open countryside through an old wooden gate. Before you is an imposing electricity pylon with is wires running up and down this lovely countryside and scarring the view.

Walk to the left of the pylon and continue straight ahead on the crest of the ridge. Now is a good time to stop and catch your breath as stretched out before you is the most fantastic view of the Cheltenham and Gloucester basin. Here too are glimpses of green hilltops in neighbouring Worcestershire and, peeping over May Hill, the mountains of southern Wales.

After 300 yards the path again divides in several directions as the "Cotswold Way" comes in from the right and left. Here you leave your path and follow the yellow arrow sign with a black dot going off slightly right and begin to drop downhill, away from the wood.

Down to your right is a farm scene straight off a postcard and beyond the blue waters of Dowdeswell Reservoir. The path is now quite steep.

Soon you have a dry stone wall on your left and yet again the paths divide at an old wooden gate. Here you turn left and enter a field through a large metal gate, now walk straight ahead. Again the views are quite staggering.

You now pick up the blue arrow signs of a "bridle way" which narrows between the hedges. At the bottom of the slope go over another stile and continue straight ahead with the fence on your left down the field. Go to the left of a telegraph pole and through a small metal gate onto a broad track; here you turn right.

The track is well used and again the views are good. Pass two farm cottages on your right and continue downhill to go through a large metal gate. At the bottom of the next field go through a small wooden gate and along the edge of a wood; this short section can sometimes get muddy.

Follow the track out of the wood as it continues to make its way down hill. Eventually it meets a minor road called Timbercombe Lane where you turn left and walk down to the busy A435 Cheltenham to Cirencester road. This is a very busy road and you need to cross it with great care. Opposite is the opulent "Cheltenham Park Hotel" and just to the right of it the "Clock Tower" public house. Although it's a very modern pub in an annexe of the old hotel, this is without doubt a pub worth finding. The menu is second to none and very reasonable and the beers are wide ranging including a "real ale" or two.

The old stocks in New Street, Charlton Kings, near the Church of St Mary.

Leaving the pub, retrace your steps over the A435 and back up Timbercombe Lane to rejoin the "bridle way" to Wistley Hill. After 150 yards the track divides three ways. Take the stony track to your left, keeping a fence on your left and climb the steady slope between the trees.

This track again can get very muddy so pick your way with care until you finally go through a large metal gate into a field and continue straight ahead. Again there are fine views of both Cheltenham and Charlton Kings on your left and Leckhampton Hill with its disused quarries back to your right.

Go through a small metal gate and follow the path as it continues to climb at a slight angle to your right. At the top of this short field, with a hedge on your left go through another small gate onto a narrow track.

Once again you are on a muddy section but this is the last one as you battle your way between the hedges to break out once again on the open slopes of Wistley Hill. Take the track to your left.

You now have a fence on your left. After 30 yards do not go through the farm gate ahead of you but continue to keep the hedge and fence on your left. This section is easy walking and the views to your left of both Dowdeswell village and its nearby reservoir are quite magnificent.

As the section ends the famous walk, the "Cotswold Way" joins you from the right. Just after this, pass under the electricity lines and at the end of the track go through a small metal gate into a field. Again the path divides and you continue straight ahead across the field following the yellow arrows with a white dot.

Pass the farm house on your left and go over a stile back into "Lineover Wood". Now stay on the track through the wood as it winds its way between the well cared for trees. This is a conservation area cared for by the "Woodlands Trust". Towards the end of this path you come to a fine example of a "basket" sometimes called a "dead hedge", a device used since ancient times to protect coppiced trees. The particular tree that this "basket" protects is a large leaved lime believed to be over 500 years old.

Continue along the path until you come to a wooden gate and stile. The "Cotswold Way" goes over this stile but here you leave it and turn back to your right and climb a steady slope on a narrow track, back into the wood.

At the top of this track you come to a series of wooden steps which you follow to the top of the hill and back to your car.

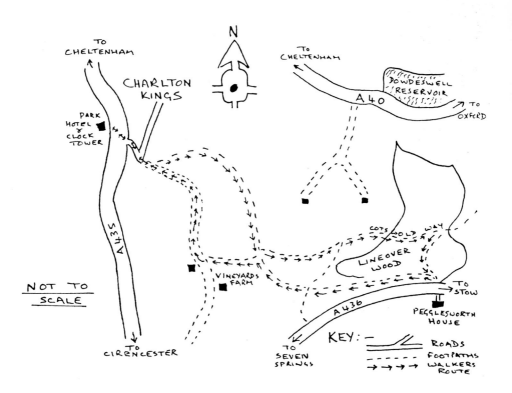

WALK 14

Pegglesworth to Dowdeswell

Distance: 3 miles
Allow: 1 1/2 hours

"A testing, short walk offering unrivalled views of Gloucestershire and beyond. A woodland walk reminiscent of Austria in parts which gives you a chance to enjoy a meal and a drink in a nice old pub before tackling the steep finish."

Pegglesworth is an area on the A436 Gloucester to Stow-on-the-Wold road mid-way between Seven Springs and Andoversford. The walk starts from the layby opposite "Pegglesworth House" over a stile that takes you into "Lineover Wood". Parking is limited in the layby and you may be forced to use the large layby some 200 yards away and walk back to the wood. Parts of the walk can get quite muddy so come prepared with appropriate footwear.

Go over the stile into the wood and immediately the path divides turn left and follow the escarpment path parallel with the road. The walking is easy and although the road is close it could already be miles away as the wood is so peaceful.

Off to your right the views very quickly open up and Cheltenham looks magnificent set in a natural basin protected by Cleeve Hill and, beyond, the Malverns.

At the end of the track drop slightly to the right, cross a stile and immediately turn right to cross another stile. Here the path again divides and you follow the yellow arrow sign indicating a path straight ahead to drop steeply down hill on a series of wooden steps.

"Lineover" after which the wood is named means "lime bank" in Anglo Saxon. The wood is 111 acres and was first recorded around 800 A.D. It's a favourite home for a wide variety of wildlife including deer, badgers, foxes and a myriad of bird life.

At the bottom of the slope the path goes over a stile and off at a slight left angle. It is still well marked at this point. Cross over another wooden stile and continue down hill just to the left of an old quarry. Now head for the far left hand corner of the field in the direction of a large electricity pylon.

It is unfortunate that the pylons and their cables detract from the beauty of this area as the next short section is quite unusual for Gloucestershire; from the layout of the land and trees you could almost be in Austria. The section is not marked with any waysigns and you need to follow it with care.

Go through an old metal gate in the corner of the field and after 10 yards turn right and go through a second metal gate. Now keep the pylon on your left and make your way down a wide track, straight ahead. Half way down the slope go through a third metal gate and continue down with the hedge on your left towards a cattle grid. You now pass under the electricity cables.

From here you get the most magnificent views of Dowdeswell village to your right, Ham Hill ahead of you and to your left the urban setting of Cheltenham. There is a thick, pine wood to your right and buzzards are commonly seen soaring over the tree tops.

Go over the stile alongside the cattle grid and follow the metalled farm track straight ahead, once again following the yellow arrow signs. At the end of this track there is a stile alongside a final cattle grid and you are now walking on a road; this is Capel Lane and leads you down to the busy A40 Cheltenham to Oxford road.

Cross over the A40 with great care and turn right, keeping to the footpath. After 400 yards you have the opportunity for a rest in the "Reservoir Inn" on your right. The inn has recently been converted and boasts a fine, inexpensive restaurant in addition to offering a wide range of beers including "real ales".

From the pub continue up the A40, using the grass verge, for about 100 yards keeping the road on your left. Now take the footpath going off to your right which is marked by a yellow arrow with a white dot. This sign indicates that you are walking on a section of the "Cotswold Way".

This next section is quite steep and can also get very muddy so take your time on it. The views are good and give you several opportunities to just stop and catch your breath.

Go over a stile and follow the arrow signs taking you slightly left. To your right is a wonderful view of Wistley Hill. Keep the hedge on your left as you climb the slope. Very soon the track narrows between the hedgerows and there is a series of wooden steps to help you on your way.

After the steps, go over a wooden stile and continue up the field keeping the fence on your left. Here is another opportunity to stop and admire the wonderful view opening up to your right.

At the top of the field go over a stile and leave the "Cotswold Way", which now goes off to your right. Do not follow it into the wood but walk up the field at a slight right angle to a stile, with a yellow arrow in the top right hand corner of the field, now having the wood on your right.

Go over the stile and climb the steep slope keeping a fence on your right. Almost at the top of this slope go over another wooden stile and continue straight ahead.

After about 20 yards, when the slope finally flattens out go into the wood on your right over a large wooden gate. Take the track going off to the left and follow it as it snakes its way gently upwards, through the trees. You are now back in "Lineover Wood" and the walking is very easy.

The path finally makes its way up to a drystone wall which you keep on your left. After a further 250 yards you arrive at the detailed information board at the top of the wood, the point that you originally entered it and your car.

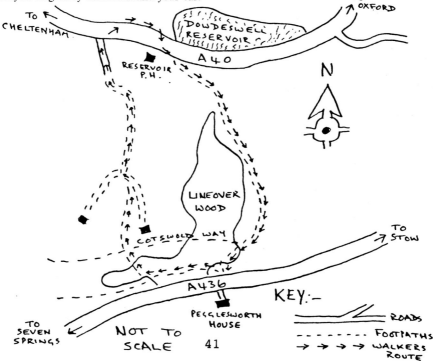

WALK 15

Seven Springs to Birdlip

Distance: 6 miles

Allow: 3 hours

"An easy stroll between two popular pubs with lush countryside offering the most magnificent views in Gloucestershire. A chance to see fields and pastures which are largely undisturbed by time".

Park your car in the large lay-by off the A436 road at Seven Springs opposite the "Seven Springs Inn". You already have a choice to make as to whether you visit the inn now or on your return. Whichever you choose you will get a warm welcome in a pub that offers a wide variety of drinks and food.

The location derives its name from the fact that here seven springs erupt into a small pool to form the head of the delightful River Churn, a tributary of the mighty Thames.

From the lay-by start your journey by turning right and with great care cross the busy road to walk along the grass verge, heading for the sign that advertises the "Seven Springs Playground". This stretch of road walking is very hazardous and stretches for about 100 yards where you leave the roadside to join a footpath on your left, having threaded your way between a metal "kissing gate" and a wooden stile.

Unfortunately the next short section has been fenced in by the farmer to keep you on a very narrow path but do not despair -there is some lovely country walking awaiting you.

After negotiating two wooden stiles the footpath divides and you need to take the one to your left. This well used footpath takes you down into the pretty little village of Coberley.

Walk down to the centre of the village and, keeping the stone cross on your right hand side, make for the little footpath directly ahead of you. Keep the three large pine trees on your left and drop down to the minor metalled road which you cross straight over.

Pass through the wooden "kissing gate" and follow the yellow arrowed footpath down the slope. Take a breather at this point to look back and admire the village behind you and the water garden on your left.

At the bottom the path crosses the newly formed River Churn and a wooden stile. Here the path divides two ways and you take the path up the slope to the right and cross another wooden stile.

Now go straight ahead, making for the farm gate in the far right hand corner where there is a third stile. Having crossed this keep close to the wooden fence on your left and make your way down the farm drive to the metalled road. Here you turn right and follow the road for some 200 yards before turning left onto a well marked "public path" which is a wide track.

After about 400 yards the track divides into two "bridle ways" marked by blue arrows. Leave the track and take the "bridle way" to your left, entering it through a wooden five bar gate.

This next stretch is a really lovely valley with wonderful open views of countryside in all directions and is flat and easy walking, passing through two more wooden farm gates.

Keep straight ahead until you reach a metal gate where the path again divides. Here you turn right on a well used path taking you up the valley as it rises, keeping the lone tree on your right.

At the top you will see a long-abandoned building which you keep on your left and join a narrow path ahead of you. Now make sure that you keep the dry stone wall on your right as you

42

cross a field and pass between the runs of a large dog kennel and cattery to join the driveway which you walk down.

The road swings left and you now pass by three large radio ariels on your left. At the crossroads ignore the turnings left and right and keep straight ahead. This is a high vantage point and offers, on a clear day, wonderful views of Bredon Hill, Cleeve Hill, the Malvern Hills, May Hill and on into Wales.

The road passes under the busy A417 Gloucester to Cirencester road to a "T" junction, where you turn right and head down to the topograph and viewpoint at Barrow Wake. Here is your chance to stay for a while and soak in the magnificent views all around you. The hills offer a great opportunity for the children to play and picnic in the warmer weather.

From here continue down the road towards Crickley Hill and your next stop at the "Air Balloon", a wonderful old pub offering an unrivalled selection of "real ales" and a variety of meals.

Leave the pub by its rear car park and, taking great care, cross the very busy A417 to a copse opposite. Here you will find a well marked footpath at the top of the bank indicating the way to Cowley. Climb the wooden stile to join the path as it snakes its way through the wood to the far right hand corner to emerge in a field.

Here you turn left on the footpath, marked with yellow arrows and head for the large white disc at the far side of the field. Cross the narrow lane and a wooden stile and again head towards another white disc across the field.

Enter the field to the left of the disc, turn right and keep the hedgerow on your right.

When you reach a wide track turn left and follow the track for some 250 yards, sweeping right as it does at a "public path" sign. Continue on the track as it passes "Cuckoopen Barn Farm" and remain on it for a quarter of a mile when it re-joins the point where you left it earlier.

Now retrace your steps down the slope to Coberley and on to your awaiting car and another chance for a pub visit at the "Seven Springs Inn"

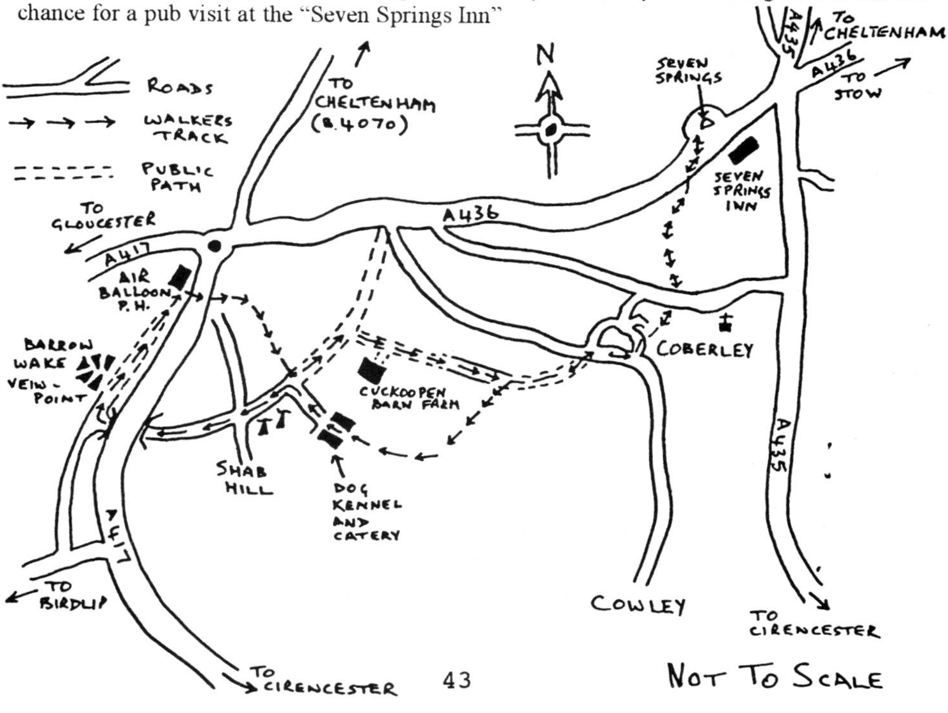

ROADS

WALKERS TRACK

PUBLIC PATH

TO GLOUCESTER

A417

AIR BALLOON P.H.

BARROW WAKE VIEW-POINT

TO BIRDLIP

SHAB HILL

DOG KENNEL AND CATTERY

CUCKOOPEN BARN FARM

TO CHELTENHAM (B.4070)

A436

N

SEVEN SPRINGS

SEVEN SPRINGS INN

TO CHELTENHAM

A436

TO STOW

A435

COBERLEY

COWLEY

TO CIRENCESTER

TO CIRENCESTER

43

NOT TO SCALE

WALK 16

Sevenhampton to Brockhampton

Distance: 2 1/2 miles
Allow: 1 1/2 hours

"A circular walk that takes you alongside the River Coln at Sevenhampton, gently up to a high ridge, offering unforgettable panoramic views, then back via Brockhampton and its friendly village pub."

Park your car in the "no through road" leading to St.Andrew's Church, Sevenhampton where your journey begins. The church, whilst typical of Norman churches all over the area, was much improved in the 15th Century with a gift from a rich wool merchant, John Camber, and has a perpendicular tower named after him.

Directly opposite the church gates enter a field on a footpath marked "Lower Sevenhampton". The well used path takes you to the far left hand corner of the field where you pass through a wooden "kissing gate". Follow the path down to your right to join the River Coln. Ignore the first bridge but climb the wooden stile and cross the second bridge to follow the path along the valley with the river on your right for about 100 yards.

Here you emerge onto a narrow metalled road with a ford on your right. Turn left and climb the small rise where you turn right at the first road junction. Now you have an opportunity to admire some lovely cottages as you make your way along the narrow road which in turn becomes a track.

Follow the "bridle way" signed through a metal gate. At the next metal gate continue straight ahead still on the "bridle way" with the tree line on your left for about 200 yards. Pass through one more gate and at the second gate enter the field on your left and continue to climb, now keeping the drystone wall on your right.

Very soon, at the top of the short rise, you meet a well defined "public path" where you turn left. Ignore the "bridle way" markings at this point. Make the most of the opportunity here to catch your breath and look back at the panoramic view below. To the left is Andoversford and an old stone quarry. To your right a tantalizing view of Winchcombe. In between the villages of Sevenhampton and Brockhampton nestling under the protective cape of Cleeve Common.

There is no shortage of nature here and in addition to all sorts of farm animals you are likely to glimpse deer, rabbit, fox, partridge and pheasants busy in their forage for food.

Stay on this track, where the walking is easy, for over half a mile until it flattens out and you are almost at the highest point on this part of the Cotswolds. Look out for a wooden footpath sign on your right marking paths to your left and right. Take the left hand path down into Brockhampton, keeping the low stone wall on your left.

Pass through a wooden gate and join the minor road that drops down into the village. Here is another opportunity to rub shoulders with some beautiful old cottages, looking much as they did in the last century.

At the bottom of the village, pass the telephone kiosk on your right and take the next turning left into a "no through road". If you have time to spare and would welcome a break then here is your chance to visit a village pub in traditional style. The "Craven Arms" is to be found on your left and offers "real ales", snacks and lavish meals.

From the pub rejoin the metalled road and follow it downhill for a few yards. Here is a well marked footpath sign pointing the way to "Sevenhampton via St.Andrew's Church". Follow the path to re-cross the River Coln through a metal gate where a yellow arrowed sign marks your route to the left.

The path now gently rises across the field towards a farmhouse in the far corner where you pass through a wooden gate. Keep the large stone wall on your right to cross one more field before entering the churchyard of St.Andrew's through a metal "kissing gate".

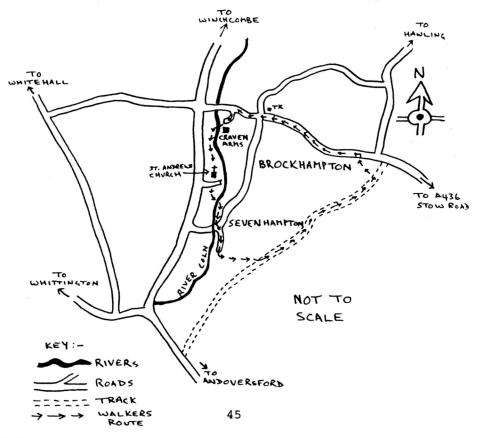

WALK 17

Siddington to South Cerney

Distance: 4 miles
Allow: 2 hours

"A pleasant, easy walk along the course of a long-abandoned canal, criss-crossing the River Churn with a choice of pubs for company".

Park your car in the small car park in the centre of Siddington opposite the turning for Bowly Crescent.

Turn left out of the car park. After 100yds turn left again onto a well signed footpath over a stile. (If you are looking to start the walk with a meal or a drink the popular pub, "The Greyhound" is just a step down the road). Your journey now takes you alongside the course of the long-abandoned Thames & Severn Canal which you keep on your left.

The canal was opened in 1789 to link the Stroud water Canal at Stroud, with the head of the navigable Thames at Lechlade, and was finally abandoned in 1927. The towers that you see alongside the canal once housed the "lengthmen" or maintenance men.

After about a mile of having the canal for company, as it criss-crosses the River Churn, it finally peters out by a house and a metalled road. Here you cross the road and continue on the footpath straight ahead. Your path veers slightly right aiming for the far right hand corner of the field.

The Round Tower

Cross the narrow metalled road to rejoin the footpath straight ahead, where the canal can once again be seen on your left. After about 250 yards take a footpath on your right which is marked by a yellow arrow and protected by a large piece of Cotswold stone.

Walk straight ahead across the field to pass under an old railway bridge and go through the metal farm gate. Now the footpath veers slightly left to the far corner of the field. Cross another stone stile and continue at the same angle to a second stile.

Now head for the churchyard wall ahead, follow it around to the left and cross a wooden fence, negotiate a metal "kissing gate" and finally a wooden gate to emerge in Church Lane, South Cerney.

Here is another opportunity to stop for a drink and a bite to eat as there is a choice of two pubs by the river bridge, the "Eliot Arms" and the "Old George Inn", both offering a wide range of excellent food and drink.

From here, cross straight over Silver Street into School Lane, to enjoy a feast of architectural delights that await you in what must be the prettiest part of the village, including a magnificently thatched village hall.

Keep the River Churn on your left and stay on this road until it ends at the entrance to a private drive. Here there is a wooden stile on your left which you cross and then turn right to climb up the slope. Keep the hedgerow on your right as you cross the field and two wooden stiles.

After the second stile the hedgerow should now be on your left and soon peters out. When it does, keep straight ahead and cross a series of wooden stiles, always heading in the same direction. The last of these stiles can sometimes be difficult to find, depending upon the season and lies below you through a gap in the hedgerow.

You are now back on the canal towpath where you turn left and follow it back for the best part of a mile to Siddington, your car and another chance to visit "The Greyhound" public house.

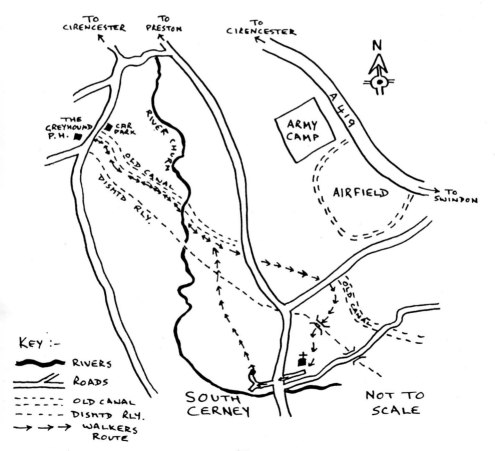

WALK 18

Stow-on-the-Wold to Broadwell

Distance: 4 1/2 miles

Allow: 2 1/2 hours

"A short easy walk with the benefit of a number of pubs, shops and cafés at the start and finish. This is a walk that takes you from the ancient market place at Stow-on-the-Wold to a fine old village with a traditional real ale pub for a half-way break."

The walk starts in the ancient market place at Stow-on-the-Wold where parking is restricted. However there is a large, free car park on the Maugersbury road where you can leave the car and make your way back to the starting point.

Start your journey outside the Whitbread public house, the "White Hart", which offers a wide range of "real ales", snacks and meals. Go through the old double door coach entrance to the left of the pub, which is a public "right of way" and signposted to the beer garden.

The path soon leaves the pub garden and becomes a road, you are now heading towards a small factory called "Cotswold Laminators Ltd".

At the first road junction turn left and keep the "Royal British Legion Club" on your right; this is Camp Gardens. After 40 yards the road sweeps left and here you turn right on a minor "no through road".

To the right is a lovely deep green valley and an open aspect towards Evenlode and on into both Oxfordshire and Warwickshire. The lane is popular with walkers and after some 200 yards you pass the two old town wells on your left. These run crystal clear and plentiful all year round.

The road eventually peters out and becomes a stone "bridle way" which is flat and easy walking. From here there are unrestricted views. This is sheep country and there are many of them around. At points, the path closes in on you and ends in an avenue of trees.

When the path meets a minor country road turn right and begin to drop down the hill. Although this is only a narrow road it is well used and you need to exercise care. There are pleasant open farmland views to the right.

At the bottom of the hill you enter the village of Broadwell as the road sweeps around to the left. Soon you come to a "T" junction and here you turn left for Donnington and Moreton-in-Marsh.

You are now in the heart of this pretty Cotswold village which boasts a fine collection of stone built cottages as well as a traditional pub, the "Fox Inn", and a most magnificent village green. The green offers an opportunity for a rest or a sandwich and the pub offers a very warm welcome.

The "Fox Inn" is a Donnington pub selling its unique "real ale" and also boasts an extensive menu. There is a beer garden at the rear of the pub and in the summer months a chance to join in with the locals in a game of "Aunt Sally". This is an old Oxfordshire garden game which is becoming very popular on the Cotswolds.

If you feel it's still too early to stop at the pub you have a second chance to visit it on this circular section of the walk.

Pass the pub on your left and continue up the road with a clear stream also on your left. After about 20 yards turn right on a public footpath again with the stream on your left and climb a slight slope. This is a beautiful section and one to be savoured on a hot sunny day. The stream is broad and clear and just beginning its journey to join the River Evenlode.

At the top of the grassy slope the path again meets a minor road where you turn right and head down hill. After 15 yards turn left into Kennel Lane, which is a "no through road". On your right is a beautifully converted "Dutch" barn and all around are Cotswold stone cottages.

Follow the road as it makes its way between the houses until it becomes a wide track and although there is little of interest you get a strong feeling here that you are right in the heart of the country.

It is still flat and easy walking. After almost a quarter of a mile there is a very broad, well marked "bridle way" on the right. Take this path.

This short section can get quite muddy so come prepared for this with appropriate footwear. At the bottom of the slope continue straight ahead through a metal gate and over the stream, keeping the hedgerow on your right.

At the top of the slope go through a wooden gate onto a driveway and walk straight ahead to cross a cattle grid and join another minor road. Here you turn right.

Again take care because these roads are well used. Here you pass between an assortment of houses and the scene is very reminiscent of a picture off a chocolate box lid. This is Chapel Street.

At the "T" junction, opposite "Broadwell Farm", turn right and this will take you back to the village green and another chance to visit the "Fox Inn". From here retrace your steps from the green up the minor road to Stow-on-the-Wold, with its shops, cafés and pubs.

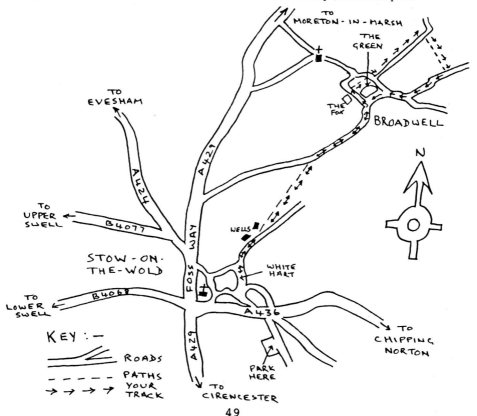

WALK 19

Twyning to Church End

Distance: 3 miles

Allow: 2 hours

"An easy, flat, circular walk taking you gently alongside the River Avon, offering unequalled views of the surrounding countryside and the wildfowl that abounds in the area. The walk starts and ends at a friendly riverside pub."

Drive right through the village of Twyning and down to the "Fleet Inn" alongside the River Avon where you can safely park off the little narrow road. This is the start and end of your journey so whether you choose to visit the pub now or after your walk you will not be disappointed. It has a true old fashioned village atmosphere and offers a wide range of beers and an extensive menu.

The river is wide and quite impressive at this point, dotted with a variety of wildlife and a small flotilla of colourful pleasure boats moored alongside its banks. Here too is a grassed picnic area offering fine views in all directions. To the left is Bredon and its famous hill and off to the right, Tewkesbury, which marks the end of the road for the Avon as it merges with its mightier brother, The Severn.

You start your journey by walking down towards the river and turning to your right at a "footpath" sign. Within a few yards cross a wooden stile and pick up the first of a series of yellow marks which take you along the river bank.

The whole walk is well marked and easy to follow. Take your time as you cross this first field to look back at the traffic pouring over the motorway bridge behind you and glory in the fact that for once you are not part of it - a fact that is far from wasted on the many anglers that you pass along this route.

At the end of this first field go through a "kissing gate" and keep straight on, all the while following the river, to cross a bridge over a small brook.

As you cross two more fields and two wooden stiles the views ahead to Tewkesbury become quite pronounced and its Abbey already begins to dominate the skyline.

Now is the time to watch your way and look out for a stile off to your right, this time showing a yellow arrow with a black dot. You will find this just before you reach the building on the opposite bank that is part of the yachting club.

Cross the stile and turn sharp right all the while following the arrowed direction marker; you are now walking back on yourself. Cross a fence and another wooden stile and take another opportunity to admire Bredon in the distance and its lovely church spire.

Go through a five bar gate and when the path divides, ignore the path to your left and continue straight ahead along a well defined track which can get muddy. The track begins to broaden as it heads directly towards the little church tower ahead of you at Church End. On your right are some beautiful lakes which belong to Church End Fishery and offer a watery home to a large number of birds.

Soon you come to a crossroads of tracks where again you go straight on. At "Church End Farmhouse" take a footpath off to your right marked Twyning Green. Ahead of you are two ponds which you loop around to the right. At the far end of the pond is a line of electricity poles which you follow to your right across the field.

Very soon you meet another well marked track and a yellow arrow and turn left. As the broad track begins to sweep left look out for a footpath off to your right in the corner of a field. Cross the wooden stile and head down the field. Ignore the footpath going off to your left half way down the field and continue straight on.

Go through an old metal "kissing gate" with a white painted top marking the route. Cross a stile and continue to follow the white markings. Pass through a large, ornate metal gate and turn sharp left, keeping the fence on your left.

Now turn left over another wooden stile, still following the yellow arrows to eventually emerge by the gates of Twyning Park where you turn right. The short road walk now takes you back to your car and the "Fleet Inn".

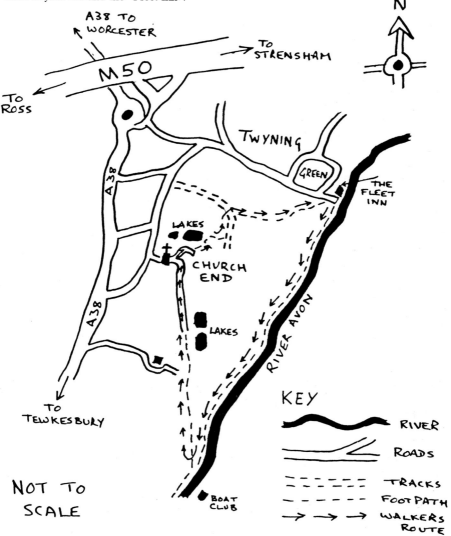

WALK 20

Windrush to Great Barrington

Distance: 3 1/2 miles

Allow: 2 hours

"A splendid stroll through open farmland, beginning and ending in one of the Cotswolds' prettiest villages. With the River Windrush for company and a pub for a rest, this is a walk that offers everything."

Park your car in the centre of Windrush village and start the walk from St.Peter's Church. The church is a fine example of the Norman style of building and is well worth visiting before you start your journey or when you end it.

Set off down the road marked "The Barringtons", keeping the church on your right.

You pass, on your left, a wonderful example of just what makes this an area of "outstanding natural beauty". The cottages are straight off a chocolate box lid. They shout quaintness and curiosity. They cry out to be photographed and frequently are.

Although you have only gone 100 yards or so, you need to take great care to follow the route, as the very first turning is unmarked. Opposite the cottage, No 27, there is a wooden gate on your right. Go through the gate and diagonally cross the field, keeping the wooden fence on your left.

The path passes between two old trees and through a metal farm gate with a yellow arrow marking the way. You now have a dry stone wall on your left and off in the distance some fine open views of the countryside.

Cross a stone stile and go straight on, this time with a hedge on your left, before crossing a wooden stile. You can now see quite clearly your path ahead as you are heading in a direct line for the church tower at Little Barrington. To your left the private park at Barrington opens up and you get your first view of the magnificent Manor House and its summer house surrounded by a large herd of grazing deer.

The walking is flat and very easy as you first cross another wooden stile and then a metal topped stile. Here you divert slightly to your right, now heading for a weather vane in the shape of a cockerel, on the top of a large barn.

Here is another wooden stile, which you cross and walk straight ahead between the buildings and right into the heart of Little Barrington.

The Stoat

This is a lovely little village and it is well worth taking stock of it as you reach the centre and turn left at a water pump and pass in front of a quite charming row of cottages. Below you is a green, interlaced by a brook - a scene quite often used as a backdrop for sales brochures.

Pass the village Post Office which is the old smithy and drop down to your right, across the green to head for a "no through road" opposite. Follow this road until it peters out and becomes a path running parallel with the River Windrush.

In the dip at the bottom turn left to cross the river using a wooden bridge and go straight ahead with a large hedge on your right. Occasionally there is a fine view of a large family house alongside the river to your right. Now cross a second bridge and follow the footpath as it passes in front of an old mill. This once proud building has seen much better days and is currently in need of some loving care.

The path now joins a well used track which takes you straight ahead and up into the village of Great Barrington. When the track meets the village road turn left and left again, keeping the war memorial on your right. Cross the road and follow the pavement down hill, keeping the estate wall on your right.

Very soon you pass the large gates protecting the Mansion House at Barrington Park and just below them the entrance to the church. It is well worth visiting the church, which is dedicated to St.Mary the Virgin and the path to it offers some fine views of the private estate.

The Mansion was built in 1737 by Lord Talbot, The Lord Chancellor and stone taken from the area not only built the mansion but was taken, down river, to London to build the present day Houses of Parliament and properties in Oxford.

Your journey continues down the hill, to the end of the estate wall where you cross the river

and have the opportunity to visit the "Fox Inn". This is a Donnington Inn offering its unique brand of "real ale" and a wide choice of food, both hot and cold. For me this is a summer pub as it has a fine garden with chairs and tables set alongside the fast flowing Windrush and is a delight.

From the "Fox Inn", climb the slope of the road and turn right at the "T" junction, following the signs for Windrush and Sherborne. You soon pass the village cricket pitch on your left which can in itself be a tempting place to stop on a nice summer's day.

If you have had enough of country walking you may choose to follow the road as it once again takes you down into the village of Windrush and back to your car. However if you would like a short adventure, after about 400 yards and as the road sweeps left and starts to climb look for a stone stile on your right and cross it.

Now head diagonally left across the field towards some large farm buildings in the distance, keeping the village on your left. The views to your right are once again quite splendid with the river below you and the deer park dominating the far banks.

Just before you reach the farm building divert slightly right to cross a stone stile and continue at an angle to your right, keeping the dry stone wall on your left.

Now you have to pick your way across a wooden causeway over a brook and climb the slope to cross a wooden stile on your left at the top. Turn sharp right and keep the wooden fence on your right before crossing a stone stile and joining a track where you turn left.

Follow the track until it joins a road and turn left to re-enter Windrush taking you back to your car.

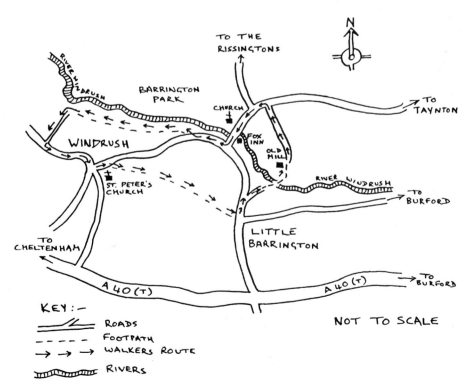

INDEX